Can Science Solve?

The Mystery
of the
Abominable
Snowman

Holly Wallace

Heinemann Library
Chicago, Illinois

Designed by **AMR**
Illustrations by Art Construction and Margaret Payne at AMR
Printed in Hong Kong, China

04 03 02 01
10 9 8 7 6 5 4 3

Library of Congress Cataloging-in-Publication Data
Wallace, Holly.
    The mystery of the abominable snowman / Holly Wallace.
       p. cm. - - (Can science solve?)
    Includes bibliographical references and index.
    Summary: Examines the existence of both the yeti and its American
"cousin," Bigfoot, describing eyewitness accounts, explanations of
the possible identities of these creatures, and hoaxes.
    ISBN 1-57572-810-9 (lib. bdg.)
    1. Yeti - - Juvenile literature. [1. Yeti.   2. Sasquatch.]
    I. Title. II. Series.
    QL89.2.Y4095   1999
    001.944- - dc21
                                             99-17396
                                                CIP

Acknowledgments
The publishers would like to thank the following for permission to reproduce
photographs:
Travel Photography/James Davis, pp. 13, 27; Eye Ubiquitous/J. Burke, pp. 9, 19;
P. Field, p. 6; D. Peters, p. 10; Fortean Picture Library, p. 21; R. Dahinden, pp. 11, 22,
25; C. Murphy, p. 28; I. Sanderson, pp. 5, 23; Jeremy Homer, p. 7; Hutchison Library,
p. 18; Mail on Sunday, p. 12; Popperfoto, pp. 8, 16; Royal Geographical Society/E.
Shipton, pp. 14, 15.

Cover photograph reproduced with permission of Ivan T. Sanderson, Fortean
Picture Library.

Every effort has been made to contact copyright holders of any material
reproduced in this book. Any omissions will be rectified in subsequent printings
if notice is given to the Publisher.

Some words are shown in bold, **like this.** You can find
out what they mean by looking in the glossary.

Contents

Unsolved Mysteries 4

Beginnings of a Mystery 6

Eyewitness Accounts 8

More Encounters 10

It's Official! 12

Looking at the Evidence 14

Bodies and Bones 16

What is the Yeti? 18

Clues from the Past 20

Fact or Fake? 22

Abominable Creatures of North America . 24

Abominable Creatures of Asia 26

In Conclusion 28

Glossary 30

More Books to Read 31

Index 32

Unsolved Mysteries

For centuries, people have been puzzled and fascinated by mysterious places, creatures, and events. Why do ships and planes vanish without a trace when they cross the Bermuda Triangle? What secrets are held by a **black hole?** Are some houses really haunted by ghosts? Does the Abominable Snowman really exist?

These mysteries have puzzled scientists who have spent many years trying to find the answers. But just how far can science go? Can science explain the seemingly unexplainable, or are there mysteries that science simply cannot solve? Read on and decide for yourself.

This book tells you about the mystery of the Abominable Snowman, also known as Yeti. It retells eyewitness accounts. It examines photographic and scientific evidence and looks at famous hoaxes. It asks if science can account for the theories about the Yeti's existence and the sort of creature it is.

What is the Abominable Snowman?

For centuries, people living in the snowcapped Himalaya Mountains of Nepal and Tibet have told stories of a huge, shaggy-haired creature. It is said to be half man and half ape. They call the creature the Abominable Snowman, or Yeti. When Western mountain climbers began to explore this area at the end of the 19th century, more stories and sightings began to emerge.

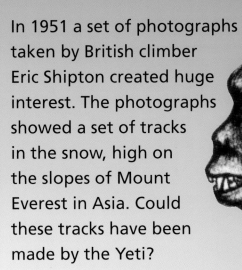

In 1951 a set of photographs taken by British climber Eric Shipton created huge interest. The photographs showed a set of tracks in the snow, high on the slopes of Mount Everest in Asia. Could these tracks have been made by the Yeti?

Finding evidence

Although concrete, scientific evidence for the Yeti has yet to be discovered, some scientists continue to search for and to question what sort of creature the Yeti could be. If the Yeti exists and turns out to be a type of ape, it will mean the scientists have found a new animal. Can science solve this mystery?

This is an artist's idea of how the Yeti might look. So far, no one has seen one close enough to know for certain.

Beginnings of a Mystery

Long before Western mountaineers first explored the Himalayas, the local Sherpa people of Nepal told ancient stories and legends of the *metoh-kangmi*. This name means "filthy or abominable snowman." The Sherpas also called this creature "Yeti." Many Sherpas claim to have seen the Yeti roaming the icy mountain passes.

The mighty Himalayas are the world's highest mountains. Large areas of the mountains have not yet been explored. Could they hide a family of Yetis?

The Yeti's lair

Yetis are said to live high in the Himalayas. This mountain range stretches for more than 1,491 miles (2,400 kilometers) across India, Pakistan, Tibet, Nepal, and Bhutan. Mount Everest is in this range. At 29,028 feet (8,848 meters), it is the highest peak on Earth. Local people fear the mountains as the Yeti's hidden lair.

Sherpa beliefs

Regardless of scientific proof, the Sherpas have no doubt that the Yeti exists. After all, Sherpas know the mountains better than anyone. They fear Yetis as an evil force in the mountains, but they respect them even more. Each year, a festival is held to drive evil spirits from Sherpa villages. One man wears a headdress of skin and hair. It is said to be a sacred Yeti **scalp**. The scalp wearer represents the spirit of the Yeti, which has been sent by the gods to punish people for their misdeeds. Eventually, the Yeti spirit is driven out of the village and evil is banished. The Sherpas like to keep Yetis at a distance. They believe that crossing a Yeti's path will bring bad luck, illness, or even death.

Other abominable creatures

The Abominable Snowman is not the only mysterious apelike creature said to survive in Earth's wild places. Many similar creatures have been sighted around the world, including appearances in North America, China, Australia, Russia, Africa, and Southeast Asia. One of the most famous creatures is Bigfoot, or Sasquatch, which may live in the forests of western North America. Since the first reports in the 19th century, there have been more than 2,000 eyewitness accounts of Bigfoot. Can they *all* be wrong?

A Sherpa man dressed in a costume is ready to take part in the annual Yeti festival in Nepal. He represents the spirit of the Yeti.

Eyewitness Accounts

Although seen many times by the Sherpas, the first recorded sightings of the Yeti were made by Europeans in the 19th century. Since then, there have been regular encounters with Yetis, mostly by mountaineers. Here are a few of their reports.

Early encounters

The earliest reference in the West to Yetis seems to be an 1832 report by B. H. Hodgson, a British diplomat in Nepal. He wrote that while he was hunting, the local people with him were frightened by a "wild man" covered in long, dark hair.

In 1889, more than 50 years later, Major L. A. Waddell was exploring the mountains. At an **altitude** of about 19,685 feet (6,000 meters), he discovered huge footprints in the snow. His Sherpa **porters** assured him that these were the tracks of a Yeti.

In 1925, N. A. Tomabazi, a member of the Royal Geographical Society in London, almost photographed a Yeti on the Zemu Glacier. It vanished before he could get it into focus.

*A Buddhist monk holds a furry **scalp** that is said to belong to a Yeti. This photo was taken on a Yeti-hunting expedition in the 1950s.*

Creature of the night

In 1970, top British mountaineer Don Whillans and his colleague Mike Thomson were leading an expedition to climb Mount Annapurna. One evening, as they set up camp, there was a commotion among their Sherpa porters. First a dark shape appeared, and then it disappeared behind a nearby ridge. That night, unable to sleep, Whillans left his tent and went outside. By the light of the moon, he spotted an apelike creature. Whillans watched the creature for ten minutes before it dropped out of sight. He was firmly convinced that he had seen a Yeti.

Could the Yeti be a hallucination seen by mountaineers climbing high in the Himalayas? Lack of oxygen at high altitudes makes it easy to imagine things.

Hallucinations and high altitude

*The higher a climber goes up a mountain, the less oxygen the air contains and the harder it is to breathe. Above 13,000 feet (4,000 meters), even the fittest mountaineers can quickly become dizzy and sick with a terrible headache and fever. The lack of oxygen may also make a climber think he or she sees things that are not really there. Some scientists who doubt that the Yeti exists say that the sightings are **hallucinations** caused by altitude sickness.*

More Encounters

Eyewitness accounts are still being reported in the Himalayas. There have also been hundreds of sightings of the Yeti's close cousins, the Alma in Russia and Bigfoot in the United States.

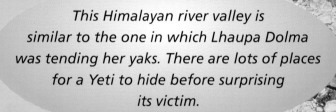

This Himalayan river valley is similar to the one in which Lhaupa Dolma was tending her yaks. There are lots of places for a Yeti to hide before surprising its victim.

Yeti attack

In 1974, a fourteen-year-old Nepalese girl, Lhaupa Dolma, had a terrifying experience. While tending her family's herd of yaks, she heard a whistling sound. Minutes later, a dark figure grabbed her from behind, pulled her hair, and threw her into the river. She was found, crying and shivering, by her brothers. Several yaks had been killed, but not by a wolf or a snow leopard, as sometimes happens in the mountains. These **predators** inflict many slicing wounds. Instead, Lhaupa Dolma's dead yaks were covered in teeth marks and had been eaten from the inside. Only the Yeti was thought to kill its prey like this.

The Russian Alma

In the mountains of Central Asia, there have been many sightings of a Yeti-like creature called an Alma. An Alma was even taken prisoner by a Russian unit of soldiers during World War II. It was reported that this "wild man" had escaped, but was later recaptured, **court-martialed,** and executed as a **deserter**.

Two more Almas were seen in the early 1960s by a hunter walking his dogs. The dogs ran off in terror. The hunter described the creatures as covered in dark hair with long arms.

Bigfoot sightings

There have been many sightings of Bigfoot, the Yeti's North American cousin. Descriptions of Bigfoot build up into a picture of a creature very similar in appearance to the Yeti. It walks "just like a man" and is covered in long, dark-brown hair. It has broad shoulders, a large chest, and hunches up as it walks. Estimates of its height range from 6 to over 9 feet (two to three meters), which is much taller than an average person. The problem is that, as with the Yeti, no real evidence has been found.

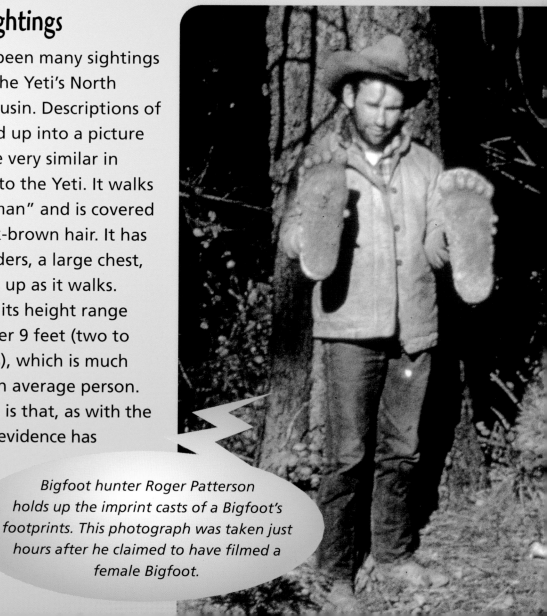

Bigfoot hunter Roger Patterson holds up the imprint casts of a Bigfoot's footprints. This photograph was taken just hours after he claimed to have filmed a female Bigfoot.

It's Official!

Interest in the Yeti continues today. Several official expeditions have tried to find or capture a Yeti. Even some hair, skin, or bones would finally convince the scientific world to take the Yeti seriously. So far, no expedition has been successful. The vastness and inaccessibility of the Himalayas makes spotting a Yeti very difficult. In addition, the many remote caves and valleys offer many places in which a Yeti could hide. Also, the Yeti is said to be **nocturnal**. It prefers to hunt at night. It would be exhausting and dangerous to try to follow a Yeti.

On the Yeti trail

In 1954, a British newspaper sent an expedition to capture or photograph a Himalayan Yeti. The expedition spent four months trekking through snow without a glimpse of the creature. However, monks in nearby Buddhist monasteries told of two different types of Yeti. One Yeti was large (a *chuti*), and one was small (a *mitey*). The monks had seen both types of Yetis several times. One monk remembered a thick, dark, yellow-brown skin kept in one monastery. He was told that it was a Yeti hide. But the monastery and the hide had been destroyed.

CHINA CRISIS OVER FOR OUR INTREPID ADVENTURER

Full speed ahead on the great Yeti hunt

Newspapers have supported many expeditions to find the Yeti. This expedition was led by British mountaineer Chris Bonington in 1988.

STOCKED UP: Bonington waits in his hotel room

In 1960, 22 scientists and mountaineers took part in the World Encyclopaedia Scientific Expedition to search for the Yeti. They were led by the famous New Zealand climber Sir Edmund Hillary. In 1953, Hillary and Sherpa Tenzing Norgay had become the first people to reach the top of Mount Everest. After six months in the mountains, the expedition had to conclude that the Yeti was a myth.

Project Yeti '88

In late 1987 and early 1988, Canadian climber Robert Hutchison organized the Yeti Research Project, nicknamed Yeti '88. Hutchison was a firm believer in the Yeti. His goal was to find and track the Yeti to its den and to study its eating, mating, and nesting habits. He also wanted to collect samples of Yeti remains so that a biological study could be made. The expedition lasted for five months. During this time Hutchison photographed many Yeti tracks, but he failed to find the creature that made them.

The Sherpas' main town in Nepal is close to Mt. Everest. Sherpas are well-known for their climbing skills. They have accompanied many Yeti-hunting expeditions.

Looking at the Evidence

Although many eyewitnesses have been top mountaineers with no motive for making up stories, science cannot rely on their accounts. Perhaps **altitude** sickness played tricks with their eyes. Perhaps the tracks were made by other creatures. Scientists must have hard proof in order to accept the idea that the Yeti exists. So, what about the evidence that has been gathered? Does it stand up to scientific analysis?

Footprints and photos

The main evidence comes in the form of hundreds of tracks in the snow that are said to belong to Yetis. In 1951, Everest explorer Eric Shipton caused a sensation when he published photographs of a trail of footprints on the Menlung Glacier. The footprints were 13 inches (33 centimeters) wide by 18 inches (46 centimeters) long. This is much larger than a human foot. The prints had three small, rounded toes and a huge big toe. They seemed to have been made by a two-legged animal. The only creatures that might leave such tracks are orangutans, which are not found in the Himalayas—or perhaps a Yeti.

The British explorer Eric Shipton examines his famous trail of Yeti footprints. He was the first person to get clear photographs of the prints.

True or false?

Many scientists dismissed Shipton's photos as fakes. But Shipton's story seemed genuine. Could a Yeti really have made the prints? Or were they made by another mountain creature?

One explanation was that the tracks were made by a bear. Bears normally walk on all fours, but sometimes to save energy as they walk through snow, they put their back paws into the prints made by their front paws. Dr. T. C. S. Morrison-Scott from the British Museum had another theory. He concluded that the prints belonged to a type of monkey called a Himalayan langur. His critics disagreed, because the langur, like most **primates**, mostly walks on all fours, and its feet have five long toes, not four as in the photograph.

A close-up of a footprint found by Shipton is shown with the head of an ice axe to give an idea of its size. Was the footprint really made by a Yeti?

Freeze-thaw

*Are footprints in the snow reliable evidence? One major problem, called the "freeze-thaw **phenomenon**," suggests not. An impression is left in the snow. It thaws during the day when the sun shines, then it refreezes at night. This causes a footprint to change shape. In this way, even quite small footprints, such as those of a mountain goat or even a human, can be made to look much larger than they actually are.*

15

Bodies and Bones

There is one piece of evidence that would convince scientists of the Yeti's existence—an actual body. Even samples of skin, hair, bones, or droppings would allow a detailed analysis to be made. Then the question of whether the Yeti exists at all could perhaps be solved. So far, though, evidence has been hard to find.

Sacred relics

The 1954 *Daily Mail* expedition made an exciting discovery. Several Buddhist monasteries claimed to own pieces of a Yeti that they worshiped as sacred **relics**. The most precious relics were Yeti **scalps**. These were long, cone-shaped, and covered in short, reddish hair.

One scalp was a definite fake. It was made from animal skins sewn together. Other scalps seemed to be in one piece. As a special favor, Sir Edmund Hillary was allowed to take a scalp to London. The hair was examined under a microscope. By comparing the hair to other known types of animal hair, the scientists found that it belonged to a Himalayan goat called a *serow*. It did not belong to a Yeti.

Today, the scientific techniques of DNA testing could be used to solve the mystery. But the monasteries guard their relics carefully. To them, these relics are sacred, no matter what science may say.

Sir Edmund Hillary arrived in London with a sacred Yeti scalp. With him is Khumbo Chumbi, a village elder from Nepal and the keeper of the scalp.

Mistaken identity

In the 1920s, Swiss **geologist** François de Loys shot and killed an extraordinary creature on the border between Colombia and Venezuela in South America. It was about five feet (one and a half meters) tall. Like the descriptions of the Yeti, it looked like a cross between a man and an ape. **Zoologists** now think that the mystery animal was, in fact, a previously unknown type of **spider monkey**. The Yeti was no nearer to being found.

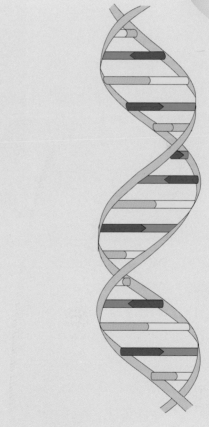

The DNA molecule has a distinctive ladder shape. It carries the biological codes that determine how an animal looks.

DNA testing

*DNA stands for deoxyribonucleic acid. It is a chemical found in the cells of every plant and animal. DNA contains the **genetic** make-up that determines everything about living things. Other than identical twins, every animal has a unique DNA profile, or pattern. This makes DNA very useful for identification. Scientists can test cells in samples of skin, hair, and blood and match them with samples from known creatures. Unfortunately, DNA testing is more useful in proving what a creature is not, rather than what it could be.*

What is the Yeti?

If the Yeti exists, what sort of creature is it? Most eyewitnesses describe a shuffling, apelike creature that is taller than a person, has shaggy hair, and walks on two legs. Could it be a new species of giant ape, unknown to science? Or a subspecies of a known ape? It might even be a new type of creature. Some scientists think it might be the descendant of a prehistoric ape that is thought to be **extinct**. It could even be a descendant of prehistoric humans. Does science rule out any of these theories?

Giant apes

Zoologists count gorillas, orangutans, and chimpanzees as among the great apes. Apes are warm-blooded mammals, belonging to the group of animals called **primates**. They have shaggy hair, broad chests, and no tail. The great apes can walk on two legs, although they usually walk on all fours. This is remarkably similar to descriptions of the Yeti.

A mountain gorilla from Zaire, Africa, is a great ape. Could the Yeti be a new, fourth species, or a subspecies of a known ape? Either would be an amazing scientific find.

None of the known great apes live in Nepal or Tibet. Orangutans are only found in Borneo and Sumatra. Gorillas and chimpanzees live in Africa. So, if the Yeti is a giant ape, it might be a new species unknown to science.

Harsh conditions

Scientifically, there is another problem. How likely is it that a giant ape could survive in the harsh conditions of the Himalayas? The answer is that it is not very likely. In winter, temperatures plummet to −4°Fahrenheit (−20°Celsius), far too cold for an ape. Food is also hard to find in winter. At this time, other mountain animals hibernate or move lower down the mountains for food. If the Yeti were among them, surely it would have been seen more often?

The chance that another great ape is yet to be found is very small. But it is not completely impossible.

High life

Some scientists argue that no animal could survive in the high mountain cold. But in summer, wild yaks climb to heights of over 16,400 feet (5,000 meters) in search of food. Their long, thick coats protect them from severe cold. In addition, as they digest food, the contents of their stomachs ferment and produce heat. It is like having a built-in heating system. If yaks can live at very high altitudes, why not Yetis?

In Nepal and Tibet, yaks are used to provide milk, butter, and hides. They also carry heavy loads.

Clues from the Past

If science rules out a giant ape, what other type of creature could the Yeti be? Could its origins lie in the distant past with a group of prehistoric apes, or could its origins possibly be with prehistoric humans?

Prehistoric primates

Gigantopithecus was a huge ape that lived in China and India about twelve million years ago. Fossilized remains seem to say that males reached heights of eight feet (two and a half meters), which is the size of a very large gorilla. In the 1950s, Dutch **zoologist** Bernard Huevelmans suggested that Eric Shipton's famous Yeti footprints may have been made by a living relative of *Gigantopithecus*. Perhaps these apes or their descendants still survive and are hidden in the mountain forests. Few scientists took Huevelman's ideas seriously. Most **paleontologists** now agree that *Gigantopithecus* became **extinct** about 500,000 years ago.

The family tree of Gigantopithecus shows its living relations.

Ancient ancestors

An even more extraordinary theory was put forward in the 1980s by the **anthropologists** Myra Shackley and Boris Porchnev. They claimed that the Yeti—and its Russian cousin, the Alma—were, in fact, prehistoric humans, descended from Neanderthal man. Neanderthal man was an early human who lived from about 200,000 to 40,000 years ago. When the direct ancestor of humans, Cro-Magnon man, appeared on Earth about 40,000 years ago, Neanderthal man seemed to vanish completely. Perhaps he was driven out by Cro-Magnon man and was forced to find safety in ever wilder and remoter places. What could be wilder than the Himalayas?

This is an artist's impression of what Neanderthal man might have looked like. Could the Yeti be descended from these early humans? It seems unlikely, but no one can say for certain that it isn't true.

Weird and wonderful

Some of the strangest theories about the Yeti have very little to do with science. They include the idea that a Yeti may be one of the Hindu holy men, called sadhus, *who journey to the mountains to* **meditate***, enduring great hardships on the way. Even odder is the link between Yetis and UFOs. There have been several reports of bright lights in the sky, followed by a sighting of a Yeti or Bigfoot.*

Fact or Fake?

Some of the photos of Yetis, Yeti tracks, and even the actual tracks themselves have since been found to be fakes. Some are cases of mistaken identity. One photo turned out to show nothing more than an outcrop of Yeti-shaped rock. Other photos are deliberate hoaxes. For example, footprints have been faked using special boots. One of the most famous fakes of all may have been a movie shot in the 1960s. It claimed to catch Bigfoot in action.

Caught on film?

On October 20, 1967, Roger Patterson, an American rancher and amateur photographer, was riding through the forest at Bluff Creek in northern California. Suddenly his horse bolted, throwing him from the saddle. When he got up and looked around, he could not believe his eyes. In the woods across the creek skulked a huge, apelike creature. Thinking quickly, Patterson grabbed his movie camera and started to film this mysterious beast.

Here is a single frame from Roger Patterson's film of Bigfoot. Some critics believe that this was a person dressed in a Bigfoot costume. Patterson refused to believe that it was a fake.

When Patterson's movie was shown on television, it caused a sensation. It showed a rather blurred picture of a creature over six feet (two meters) tall. It had reddish-brown hair, long swinging arms, and an upright walk. At one point, the creature stopped and looked over its shoulder, straight into the camera. Patterson also collected plaster casts of footprints from the site. Was this truly the legendary Bigfoot, or was the film a clever fake?

Many of the scientists who have analyzed the film claim that it was a fake, though they cannot prove it. They insist that the Bigfoot is a man dressed up in a furry ape costume— even claiming to see a zipper on the costume. Others are not so sure. After all, Patterson himself seemed completely genuine. He had no motive for faking the movie. Perhaps he was the victim of an elaborate hoax? The controversy will continue.

The Minnesota Iceman, shown here in a drawing, was a clever hoax. Even scientists were convinced it was real.

IVAN T. SANDERSON.

The Minnesota Iceman

In June 1969, a report appeared in an American newspaper. It told of a girl who claimed that she had been attacked by a Bigfoot in some woods in Minnesota. She had only escaped by shooting the creature in the right eye.

*Apparently, the Bigfoot corpse had been frozen in a block of ice and became part of a touring exhibition. Its "owner" was a showman called Frank D. Hansen. Even some scientists were taken in by the "iceman." Two respected **zoologists** who saw the body were convinced that it was indeed that of a previously unknown type of early human. Later, the "iceman" was discovered to be a brilliantly realistic model made of rubber and polystyrene.*

Abominable Creatures of North America

The Yeti is not the only unknown, apelike beast spotted in the world's wild places. Many similar creatures have been seen all over the world. If any of these could be scientifically proven to exist and identified, perhaps the Yeti could be identified, too.

This map shows where in the Americas Yeti-like creatures have been sighted.

SASQUATCH

BIGFOOT

Bigfoot in the United States

In 1924, miners working in the mountains in Washington State saw a large, apelike creature peering out from behind a tree. One miner shot at it, and it ran into the forest. That night the miners found themselves under siege. A group of the creatures hurled rocks at their hut and pounded on the roof and doors. The next day the miners abandoned the site. The creature became known as Bigfoot.

Since then, there have been many sightings of Bigfoot. About 1,000 sightings were reported between 1818 and 1980. They have been **collated** in a book called the *Bigfoot Casebook*. Many footprints have also been discovered. In 1995, a film crew in California claimed, at last, to have caught Bigfoot on videotape. At first, they thought the creature was a huge, shaggy bear. But this was no bear. Its face was too human, and it walked like an ape.

But scientists still do not have the proof they need—an actual body. Until that is found, scientists will remain **skeptical**. If Bigfoot does exist in the forests, it cannot live alone. There must be a group for breeding. Why, then, when the forests are regularly used by walkers, hunters, foresters, and fishermen, has no one found any remains? How has Bigfoot stayed so well-hidden? We may never know.

Sasquatch in Canada

In Canada, Bigfoot is called Sasquatch, after a local Native American word meaning "wild man of the woods." One of the most remarkable Sasquatch stories happened in 1924. A construction worker, Albert Ostman, was camping in the mountains of British Columbia, Canada. He was looking for gold. He claims that one night he was kidnapped by a Sasquatch and taken to its family cave. He spent six days with them. Then seizing his chance, he fired his rifle and made his getaway. For more than 30 years, Ostman kept silent about what had happened to him. Then in 1957, he told his story to writer John Green, author of a book called *On the Track of the Sasquatch*. When asked by Green why he had kept silent for so long, Ostman replied that he thought no one would believe him.

Albert Ostman claimed to have been kidnapped by a group of Sasquatches and held prisoner in their cave.

Abominable Creatures of Asia

In the mountains of Central Asia, there are reports of a Yeti-like creature called an Alma. In the mountains of northern China, a wild man, called Xucren, has been sighted, and in Sumatra, an apeman called Orang-pendek is said to live in the rain forest. Although they are called other names, the descriptions seem to share the characteristics of Bigfoot.

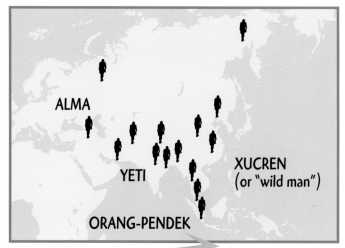

This map shows where in Asia Yeti-like creatures have been sighted.

Wild man in China

A creature similar to the Russian Alma has been sighted in the mountains of northern China. In June 1977, a man named Pang Gensheng was chopping wood when he saw a "hairy man." He was about six feet (two meters) tall with a sloping forehead and deep-set, black eyes. His body was covered in dark brown hair. His long arms hung to below his knees.

That same year, the Chinese Academy of Sciences sent an expedition to search for the "wild man." They collected casts of footprints, samples of hair, droppings, and many more eyewitness accounts. From this evidence, they concluded that the creature must be an unknown species of **primate** and quite possibly a descendant of *Gigantopithecus*.

Orang-pendek in Sumatra

Another apeman called Orang-pendek, or the "short man," is said to live in the dense rain forests of Sumatra. In the early 1990s, a team of scientists funded by the conservation organization **Flora** and **Fauna** International set out to find the animal. In 1993, one team member had a clear view of an Orang-pendek when it stepped onto the path right in front of her. Local people have been encountering the creature for years and many footprints have been discovered. The footprints show that the creature walks on two feet.

Hard evidence is difficult to find, because in the forest, a dead body can be eaten away overnight by bacteria, fungi, and scavenging animals. But the team was convinced that there is something there, possibly an unknown subspecies of orangutan, the forest's most famous inhabitant. The forest is one of the richest **habitats** on Earth. There is plenty of food to support a group of large apes. Also, much of the forest is still unexplored. The chances of survival are much better here than in other regions.

Could the orangutan be related to the Orang-pendek, or "short man," an unknown species of ape? Scientists studying the animals are sure that there is a strong link.

In Conclusion

Can science solve the mystery of the Abominable Snowman? Without an actual body or other concrete evidence to examine, most scientists seem unwilling to admit that such a creature exists. True, there are the eyewitness accounts, photographs, casts of footprints, and even fleeting glimpses of a mysterious creature captured on film. But many of these have been proven to be fakes. Others may not be reliable.

An unknown animal?

If the Yeti does exist, it seems most likely to be a new species of ape or an unknown subspecies of a known ape. Either would be a very exciting discovery for science. Either could be possible. New and unknown creatures are discovered all the time in remote and unexplored parts of the world. However, an ape would need plenty of food and shelter. Scientists say the mountains of Nepal simply do not provide enough of either.

Could this be the face of the Abominable Snowman? Scientists are still trying to find out. This fantastic creature remains one of the greatest mysteries of our time.

What do you think?

Now that you have read about the Abominable Snowman and the possible explanations for it, can you draw any conclusions? Do you believe that Yetis and similar creatures could exist? Do you have any theories of your own?

What about eyewitness accounts? Do you think they are reliable, or were they **hallucinations** caused by lack of oxygen? Could any of the tracks have genuinely been made by a Yeti? What about the photographs and movies? If they were not fakes, what did they show?

Try to keep an open mind. Remember, if scientists throughout history had not investigated things that appeared at first strange or mysterious, many important scientific discoveries would never have been made.

Glossary

altitude height

anthropologist scientist who studies how people live and behave, both in modern times and in the past

black hole region of space where gravity is so strong that not even light can escape from it

collate to put together

court-martial trial in a military court, in which members of the armed forces are charged with committing a crime

deserter member of the armed forces who has left without permission

extinct plant or animal that has died out forever

fauna animals

ferment to chemically change

flora plants

genetic having to do with a plant or animal's genes, which are the chemical codes in plants and animals' cells that determine what they will be like

geologist scientist who studies rocks to find out about the history of Earth

habitat place where an animal or a plant lives

hallucination sight, sound, or event that appears real but is not

meditate to think quietly, to have deep and serious thought

nocturnal active during the night

paleontologist scientist who studies fossils in order to understand prehistoric life

phenomenon extraordinary or exceptional occurrence

porter person who is hired to carry heavy loads

predator animal that lives by feeding on other animals

primate a type of the highest order of mammals that includes human beings, monkeys, apes, and lemurs

relic part of a holy person's, or animal's, body or belongings that is kept after death as an object of worship or respect

scalp skin on top of the head with the hair attached

skeptical questioning the truth of theories

spider monkey type of agile, long-limbed monkey that lives in Central and South America. They use their long, grasping tails as an extra arm for climbing.

zoologist scientist who studies animals

More Books to Read

Antonopulos, Barbara. *Abominable Snowman*. Austin, Tex.: Raintree Steck-Vaughn, 1996.

Gaffron, Norma. *Bigfoot: Opposing Viewpoints.* San Diego, Cal.: Greenhaven Press, Inc., 1989.

Innes, Brian. *Giant Humanlike Beasts.* Austin, Tex.: Raintree Steck-Vaughn, 1999.

Landau, Elaine. *Yeti, Abominable Snowman of the Himalayas.* Brookfield, Conn.: Millbrook Press, Inc., 1993.

Smith, Roland. *Sasquatch.* New York: Hyperion Books for Children, 1998.

Wayne, Kyra P. *Quest for Bigfoot.* Wayne, Wash.: Hancock House Publishers, 1996.

Index

Africa   7, 18, 19
Alma   10, 11, 21, 26
bear   15
Bigfoot   7, 10, 11, 23–25
Canada   25
chimpanzee   18, 19, 20
China   7, 20, 26
Cro-Magnon man   21
DNA   16, 17
Dolma, Lhaupa   10
Gigantopithecus   20, 26
gorilla   18, 19, 20
Hillary, Sir Edmund   13, 16
Himalayas   4, 6, 9, 10, 12, 19, 21
Huevelmans, Bernard   20
langur   15
Menlung Glacier   14
Minnesota Iceman   23
monks   8, 12, 16
Mount Everest   5, 6, 13, 14
Neanderthal man   21
Nepal   4, 6, 7, 8, 10, 13, 16, 19, 28
Norgay, Tenzing   13
North America   7, 24
Orang-pendek   26, 27
orangutan   14, 18, 19, 20, 27
Ostman, Albert   25

Patterson, Roger   11, 22–23
Russia   7, 10, 11, 26
Sasquatch   7, 24, 25
Sherpas   6–9, 13
Shipton, Eric   5, 14–15, 20
South America   17
spider monkey   17
Sumatra   19, 26, 27
Tibet   4, 6, 19
UFOs   21
United States   10, 24
World Encyclopaedia Scientific
  Expedition   13
Xucren   26
yak   10, 19
Yeti
  appearance   4, 8, 11, 17, 18, 23,
                                     24, 26
  expeditions   12–13, 16
  footprints   5, 8, 11, 13, 14–15,
                           20, 22, 23, 27
  habits   10, 12, 13
  scalp   7, 8, 16
  sightings   7–11, 21, 22, 24–27
Yeti Research Project   13
Zemu Glacier   8